The Sky So High

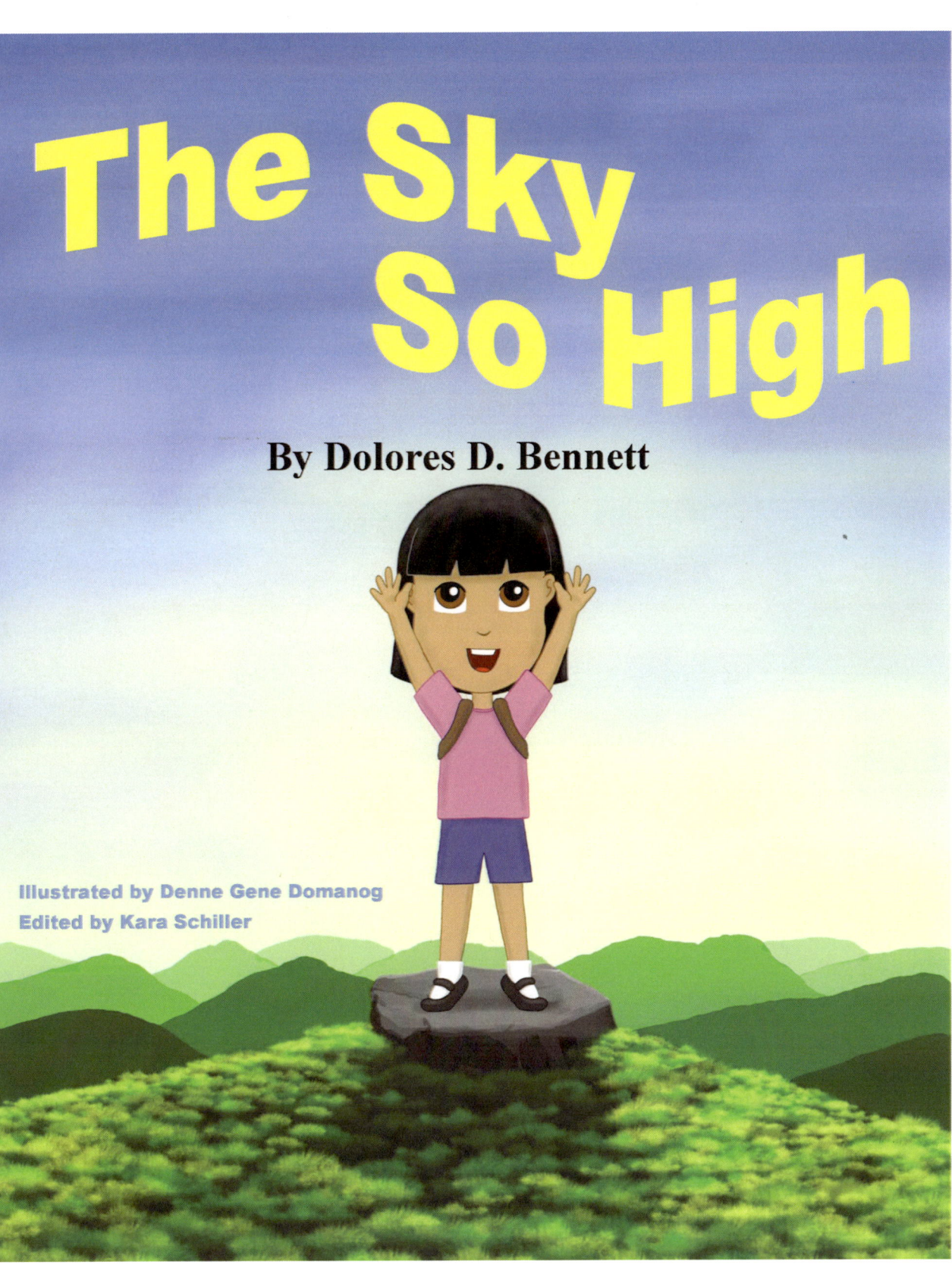

© 2022, 2024 by Dolores D. Bennett

"Someday I will climb you, high mountain. I will stand on top of you and you will help me reach the sky," Little D said as she gazed into the distance.

Her thoughts were interrupted by her grandfather. "Little D, are you ready for your first day of school?" he called.

"Yes I'm ready, Grandpa!" she answered.

On her way to school, Little D pointed at the high mountain and asked, "What's on top of that mountain, Grandpa?"

"Wild, sweet blueberries!" he responded. "When I was young, we would climb that mountain to pick blueberries and then play hide-and-seek in the meadow."

One Friday afternoon, during recess, Little D was swinging on the rings when she overheard a group of older kids talking about going to the mountain.

"You mean that mountain?" she interrupted, pointing.

"Yes!" said Ting, one of the girls, who also happened to be little D's neighbor. "You want to come along?" she asked, jokingly.

"Yes!" Little D responded enthusiastically.

Ting was surprised Little D had said yes, and was about to tell her that she'd only been joking, but it was too late. The bell rang and Little D ran back to her classroom.

On Saturday morning, Little D wrapped three small sweet potatoes to take with her for lunch.

She did all her chores without being told.

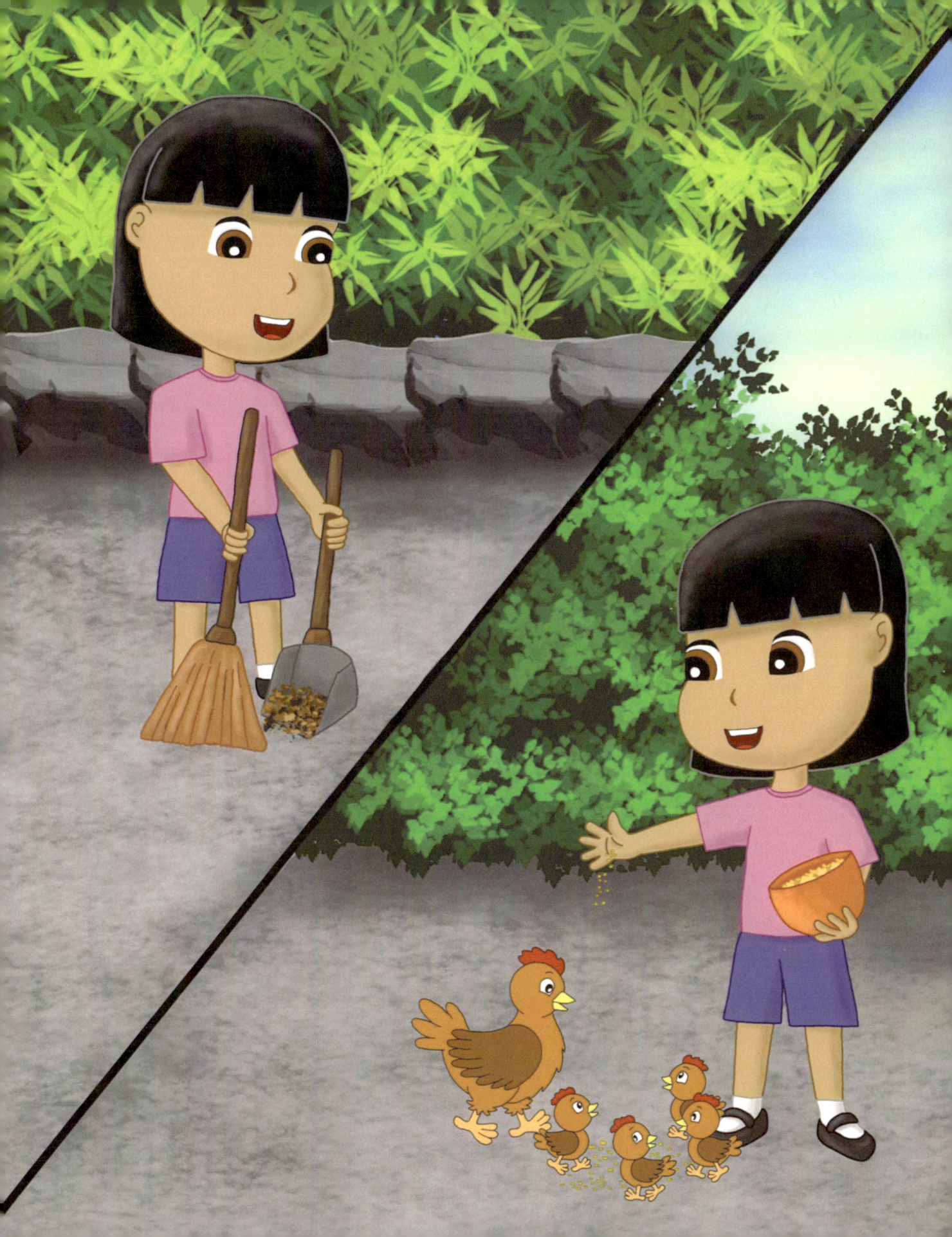

After she had let the chickens out and fed them, she peeked into the kitchen and shouted, "Bye Grandpa, I'm going to pick blueberries!"

Her grandfather looked up to respond, but Little D had already run off.

When Ting discovered Little D waiting for her on her porch, she couldn't say no, so she took her along.

Upon reaching the mountaintop, Little D lifted her arms above her head and stretched her fingers as high as she could to reach the sky... but the sky was still too high!

Her arms dropped with disappointment. It had not worked!

Little D did not tell anyone about her disappointment because she was afraid to be laughed at. Instead, she lay down in the soft grass and looked up at the sky. "Maybe I need to climb a taller mountain to reach the sky," she thought sadly.

"Come on Little D, we don't have all day to pick blueberries!" Ting called. She came running up and helped Little D to her feet.

"Poor thing, she must be tired," Ting thought.

When Little D saw all the bushes full of ripe, juicy blueberries, her disappointment melted away and she got busy picking them with the rest of the children.

When Little D reached home that afternoon, her grandfather was relieved to see her. "Where did you go?" he asked.

"I climbed the mountain with the big kids," she said looking down. "Here, I brought you some blueberries that I picked," Little D said, handing him a tiny bag of blueberries.

"Is this all you got?" he asked, smiling.

"I ate most of it because I was hungry," she said sadly, without smiling back.

"What's wrong Little D? Aren't you glad you finally got to climb the mountain and see it for yourself?" he asked.

"I could not reach the sky, Grandpa," Little D admitted, "I thought I'd be able to reach it, but I'm still too little." Tears began to stream down her face.

"You should not cry Little D, you should be happy," he said. "Even if you weren't able to reach the sky today, you were able to reach a certain height – a type of sky – that not all children your age have reached."

Little D wiped her eyes. "What sky did I reach Grandpa?" she asked.

Her grandpa lifted her into his lap and explained, "Today, you touched the sky of knowledge. You learned that you can't reach the big blue sky from the top of that mountain."

Little D nodded and Grandpa went on, "You also touched the sky of experience. Not everyone has gotten to experience a hike up a beautiful mountain with friends, and the chance to pick fresh, wild blueberries."

Little D grinned. "Thank you Grandpa!" she said. Suddenly, her day felt as though it had been very special, indeed.

"...the lips of knowledge are a precious jewel"

Proverbs 20:15